D1443153

WOMEN DOCTORS AND NURSES OF THE CIVIL WAR

LESLI J. FAVOR, PhD

The Rosen Publishing Group, Inc., New York

OREGON TRAIL SCHOOL LIBRARY
CASPER, WYOMING

For Jennifer

Published in 2004 by The Rosen Publishing Group, Inc.
29 East 21st Street, New York, NY 10010

Copyright © 2004 by The Rosen Publishing Group, Inc.

First Edition

All rights reserved. No part of this book may be reproduced in any form without permission in writing from the publisher, except by a reviewer.

Publisher Cataloging Data

Favor, Lesli J.
Women Doctors and nurses of the Civil War/by Lesli J. Favor.
    p. cm.—(American women at war)
Includes bibliographical references and index.
Summary: This book profiles American women who served as doctors and nurses in the Civil War.
ISBN 0-8239-4452-2
1. United States—History—Civil War, 1861–1865—Medical care—Juvenile literature 2. United States—History—Civil War, 1861–1865—Women—Juvenile literature 3. United States—History—Civil War, 1861–1865—Biography—Juvenile literature 4. Military nursing—United States—History—19th century—Juvenile literature [1. United States—History—Civil War, 1861–1865—Medical care 2. Nurses 3. Physicians 4. Women—Biography]
I. Title II. Series
2004

973.7'75—dc21

Manufactured in the United States of America

On the front cover: In this undated illustration, Federal nurses care for soldiers on the battlefield. Thousands of women served in the U.S. Army during the American Civil War, while many others volunteered.
On the back cover: Vials containing medicine used to treat injured or maimed soldiers.

Contents

INTRODUCTION

The American Civil War remains the bloodiest and most divisive conflict in the history of the United States. At the Battle of Gettysburg, the death toll shot to 43,000, higher than it ever had—or has since—for a single battle in American history. At the Battle of Antietam, 22,720 men were recorded as dead, wounded, or missing. More soldiers died on that day than were lost on any other day in the nation's military history. It was not just casualties that ravaged the country but also conflict over economic, political, and moral ideals. The

North, morally opposed to slavery but economically dependent on the industry and trade it generated, held interests conflicting with the South's economic dependence on agricultural enterprises largely fueled by slave labor. One by one, eleven Southern states seceded from the Union, forming the Confederate States of America. They were, in order of secession, South Carolina, Mississippi, Florida, Alabama, Georgia, Louisiana, Virginia, Texas, North Carolina, Tennessee, and Arkansas.

Confederate troops fired the first shots of the four-year war on April 12, 1861, at Fort Sumter, South Carolina. After the first few battles were fought, both sides faced a dawning realization: They desperately needed doctors and nurses to care for injured soldiers. Fannie Beers, a Southern nurse, described the arrival of 200 soldiers at a makeshift hospital.

> They came, each revealing some form of acute disease, some tottering, but still on their feet, others borne on stretchers. Exhausted by forced marches over interminable miles of frozen ground or jagged rocks, destitute of rations, discouraged by failure, these poor fellows had cast away one burden after another until they had not clothes sufficient to shield them

from the chilling blasts of winter . . .
Barefooted, their feet were swollen
frightfully, and seamed with fissures so
large that one might lay a finger in them.
These were dreadfully inflamed, and
bled at the slightest touch; others were
suppurating [forming or discharging pus]. . .
Their hands were just as bad, covered
with chilblains and sores.[1]

These soldiers were bedded down on straw-filled mattresses and, when the mattresses ran out, on straw, "littered down as if for horses."[2] In field hospitals, conditions could be far worse, with blood, human waste, mud, and even amputated limbs covering the ground where surgeons and nurses worked and where the wounded lay.

At the time, nursing was not an organized profession, and no training courses for nurses were in place. Men trained as doctors, and women had always tended the sick in their own and their neighbors' families. Only recently had women been admitted to medical colleges. By 1861, just a few women had graduated as doctors, and they found it nearly impossible to convince military authorities to commission them. As a result, countless women who provided medical care in army hospitals, field hospitals, and makeshift facilities were volunteers.

In the North, more than 3,000 women worked as paid army nurses, and 2,000 others worked as volunteers or as affiliates of the Sanitary Commission. In the South, thousands more women volunteered as nurses, although the Confederacy did not have an organized system of training or placing them.

On both sides of the conflict, these women faced unimagined horrors—stinking piles of amputated limbs, soldiers with abdominal wounds who

When South Carolina seceded from the Union, Fort Sumter remained loyal to the United States. The Civil War began when negotiations failed and the newly formed Confederates took the fort by force. Pictured above is a painting of the chaotic battle.

held their own intestines in with their hands, shattered bones, and crushed skulls. At the battle-front, open areas were the sites of field hospitals, while in cities such as Washington and Richmond, almost every available building was eventually used as a hospital.

In cities and towns, women provided a huge portion of the medical care, often taking soldiers into their homes, using spare bedrooms, parlors, attics, and hallways as sick wards. As a result, women on both sides of the conflict emerged with a newfound awareness of their capability to work outside the traditional sphere of the home. These women helped fuel the women's rights movement that gained momentum in America in the latter nineteenth century. Heroes such as Clara Barton inspired countless women to seek professional medical training. The Civil War, then, is more than a narrative of the struggle over slavery. It is also a narrative of an awakening of women to the field of medicine and the larger world.

DOROTHEA DIX

By all accounts, Dorothea Dix was a controversial figure as she carried out her duties as superintendent of female nurses of the Union army. Her brusque, no-nonsense manner, while generally effective, inspired reactions varying from anger to awe. On one occasion, she descended upon an army hospital and began a routine inspection without a word to introduce herself to the doctor in charge. In a huff, the man finally demanded to know who she was and why she dared to tell him what to do in his own

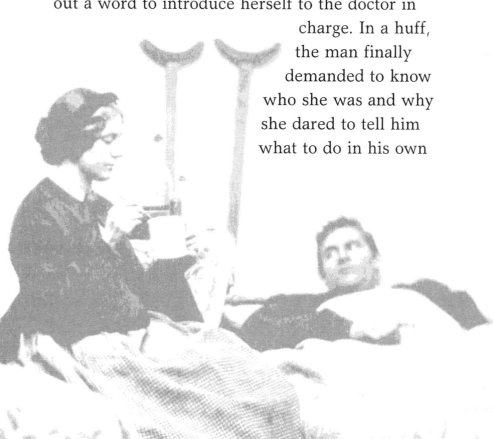

A portrait of Dorothea Dix reflects the serious-minded woman that most people reported her to be. Dix's strong commitment to basic cleanliness in hospitals and humane treatment of patients inspired other reforms such as the ones that took place in American prisons.

hospital. She replied with authority, "I am Dorothea L. Dix, Superintendent of Nurses, in the employ of the United States."[1]

To Dix, her answer said it all: She wielded authority granted by the U.S. secretary of war, Edwin Stanton, and commanded the ranks of women nurses for the entire Union army. She was a force to be reckoned with, demanding the best of herself and others—not just those she supervised but all medical personnel she encountered.

Born on April 4, 1802, in Hampden, Massachusetts (present-day Maine), Dorothea Lynde Dix was the oldest of three children. She lived the first dozen years of her life in New England, mostly in the thickly wooded terrain of northern Massachusetts. Her father, Joseph, tried his hand first at farming and then at preaching. Her mother, Mary, was a semi-invalid who spent much of her time depressed. At age six, Dorothea cared for her brothers, four-year-old Joseph and newborn John Wesley. When her father brought home piles of printed religious tracts to be folded and sewn together by hand, she was required to do this chore as well.

At age twelve, having grown to despise what seemed to her a grueling and loveless life, Dorothea showed up on her grandmother's doorstep in Boston. Two years later, having clashed wills with her grandmother, she went to live with her grandmother's sister, Sarah. She was much happier there. Soon, the fourteen-year-old Dorothea became a teacher in a girls' school. Still, the harshness of her life, the inability of her mother to care for her, and the stern rigidity of her grandmother all left a lasting impression on Dix's character. She said once, "I never knew childhood."[2] As an adult, Dix often appeared to others as stern, cold, and sometimes fearsome.

Dix did not discover the true passion of her life until, in 1841, she observed the treatment of mentally unstable and insane people. Chained in small cells, they slept on the musty straw-covered floor, which also served as table and toilet. From this time until the outbreak of the Civil War, Dix devoted herself wholeheartedly to educating prison officials, lawmakers, and the public about the needs and rights of the mentally ill. Over the next forty years, she traveled throughout the United States and Canada, inspecting insane asylums and prisons and filing reports with legislators. In fifteen states and in Canada, her reports prompted the establishment of government hospitals for the mentally ill.

In 1861, at age fifty-nine, Dix had accomplished remarkable reforms in the care of the mentally ill. But when the Civil War broke out, she identified a new area needing her service—the care of sick and wounded Union soldiers. She volunteered to head up the female nursing corps of the Union army, and on June 10, 1861, Edwin Stanton appointed her superintendent of female nurses for the Union army.

Dix approached her new role with the same vigor she had demonstrated in her previous campaigns. She had encountered resistance to her earlier reform efforts, and she encountered resistance again in her efforts to place women nurses in military hospitals. To many, the idea of a woman nurse seeing soldiers in various stages of undress was shocking. Just as alarming was the thought that "gentlewomen" would nurse soldiers from all walks of life—ruffians as well as gentlemen—and that some men might use the situation to make improper advances. Adding to this fear was the fact that it was necessary for nurses to tend to soldiers confined in beds—the most improper setting imaginable by many. As if these objections weren't enough, Dix worried, with good reason, that society would question the morals of young, attractive, unmarried women who volunteered to nurse.

Once a headquarters for British general Cornwallis during the Revolutionary War, this building was transformed into a hospital by Dorothea Dix. Dix was a skilled manager and was able to successfully run hospitals and schools the way she saw fit.

UNITED STATES SANITARY COMMISSION

The U.S. Sanitary Commission was a civilian organization established in July 1861 to help meet the needs of the Union army. Local branches sprang up all over the Northern states, fueled by volunteer efforts of women and men. Included in the Sanitary Commission's duties were collecting and shipping supplies to troops; raising money for the war effort; collecting donations of clothing, bandages, and other supplies; and organizing medical care for sick and wounded soldiers. Since the federal government founded the Sanitary Commission, it also appointed key staff positions. Dorothea Dix received her appointment as superintendent of female nurses for the Sanitary Commission from the U.S. secretary of war, Edwin Stanton. In 1862, Surgeon General Dr. Joseph K. Barnes, newly appointed by President Abraham Lincoln, declared that at least one-third of army nurses should be female.

In her new job, Superintendent Dix interviewed female applicants, ensured they received training, and assigned them to military hospitals. She devised her own set of criteria for evaluating, hiring, and supervising the women nurses. In her typical no-nonsense fashion, Dix stated that only women who were at least thirty years old and plain-looking need apply. Moreover, while at work the nurses had to dress in plain brown or black dresses with no frills such as ribbons, hoop skirts, or jewelry. Early on, she earned the nickname "Dragon Dix" as a result of these strict requirements and guidelines.

Office of Superintendent of Women Nurses,

Washington, D. C., January, 1864.

Miss Ella E. Wolcott having furnished satisfactory evidence of her qualifications for the position of a "Nurse" in the employment of the Medical Department U. S. A., is approved.

Superintendent.

Ella Louise Wolcott, a woman who was related to Oliver Wolcott (one of the signers of the Declaration of Independence), continued her family's patriotic standards by applying to be a nurse. Here is her commission, signed by Dorothea Dix, which authorizes her to be a Union nurse.

DR. ELIZABETH BLACKWELL

When Elizabeth Blackwell (1821–1910) graduated from Geneva Medical College in New York in 1849, she made history as the first woman doctor of modern times. In April 1861, Blackwell realized the Union army had two needs she could help meet: gathering medical supplies and finding medical care workers. Right away she organized the Women's Central Association for Relief (WCAR) to collect and deliver supplies to troops. A few months later, WCAR was absorbed into the newly formed U.S. Sanitary Commission. Blackwell also headed the training program for female army nurses, sending women to various New York hospitals—including her own infirmary—for instruction in medical care. After the nurses' training, Blackwell sent the women to Dorothea Dix in Washington, D.C., to receive their assignments in army hospitals.

Women whom Dix hired received $12 per month. While the paycheck was welcome, especially considering the great number of volunteers who received no pay at all, it was the (male) surgeons who received the large paychecks of up to $150.

At first the Sanitary Commission's plan for the nurses was that they would staff the hospitals in the Washington, D.C., area, away from the actual fighting. Here, nurses washed wounds, changed bandages, administered medications, washed patients' faces and hands, and served meals. Before long, however, the need for nurses in field hospitals ballooned. In response, women nurses began traveling to field hospitals to tend the sick and wounded there.

Dix was sometimes criticized for her inflexible approach to military nursing, and historians have described her as sour-minded. For instance, she was intolerant of volunteer nurses working at hospitals if they had not obtained their positions through the U.S. Sanitary Commission—in other words, if they were not under her control. When she found civilian nurses in an army hospital, she attempted to get them sent home, regardless of the hospital's need for their services.

Despite criticisms of her personality and some of her decisions, Dix blazed ahead. She did what she was charged to do, including organizing and administering a network of medical care for Union soldiers. "Dix's job would have been difficult even for someone with a more agreeable personality," writes Ina Chang in *A Separate Battle: Women and*

This is the Richmond headquarters of the U.S. Sanitary Commission, an organization founded in 1861 to improve the conditions of the Union army camps. The general secretary of the commission was Frederick Law Olmstead, who also designed New York City's Central Park. Olmstead was credited as the commission's chief organizer and helped the Union army staff field hospitals and raise funds and supplies.

the Civil War. "She was responsible for screening thousands of nursing applicants, and she had to work with officials and surgeons who resented her authority. Even though her requirements for joining the nursing corps were rigid and she may have rejected very able women simply because they looked too stylish, she succeeded in sending out a clear message: Nursing was serious work."[3]

From her appointment in 1861 through the end of the war, Dix served as superintendent, working without pay at her own request. After the war, she returned to her humanitarian work for the mentally ill. She continued to campaign for better treatment of the mentally ill until her death in 1887, at the age of eighty-five.

PHOEBE YATES PEMBER

2

At Chimborazo Hospital in Virginia, Phoebe Yates Pember had a problem with rats. Not rodents, exactly, but soldiers who feigned injury or illness to avoid returning to active duty. They were dubbed "hospital rats" since they were as difficult to get rid of as the four-legged kind. To many of these hangers-on, the hospital's store of whiskey had great appeal. At one point, a hospital rat by the name of Wilson attempted to force Pember to give him and his friends liquor. After grabbing her by the shoulder and speaking roughly, he received quite a shock when she reached into her pocket and cocked a pistol she kept there. For the time being, at least, Pember rid herself of a few rats.

Phoebe Yates Pember was born on August 18, 1823, to Jewish parents, Jacob Clavius Levy and Fanny Yates Levy. She was the fourth of seven children. A well-to-do Southern family, the Levys resided in Charleston, South Carolina. Phoebe's father was known for his literary interests, and according to one of his great-granddaughters, he was "a gentleman of leisure."[1] Little is known of Phoebe's early education. Like other young ladies of wealthy families, she may have studied with tutors at home. Later, she may have gone to a finishing school up north. Perhaps notable in light of her wartime hospital service, Phoebe had no formal medical training. She married Thomas Pember, a Boston gentleman, some time before 1860, but soon after the outbreak of the war, he died of tuberculosis. Pember returned to her parents' home, and by the following year, they were living in Marietta, Georgia.

In Marietta, Pember became acquainted with Mrs. George W. Randolph, wife of the Confederate secretary of war. In November 1862, Mrs. Randolph asked Pember to serve as matron in Chimborazo Hospital. Pember later described the idea as "rather a startling proposition to a woman used to all the comforts of luxurious life."[2] She worried that "such a life would be injurious to the delicacy and refinement of a lady [and] that her nature would become deteriorated and her sensibilities blunted . . . "[3] Despite her misgivings, she took the post and reported for duty on December 18, 1862. Her pay "was almost nominal from the depreciated nature of the currency," and matrons such as herself "had no official recognition, ranking even below the stewards from a military point of view."[4]

Located at the western edge of Richmond, Virginia, Chimborazo Hospital had been taking in wounded Confederate soldiers for nearly a year.

As the Civil War continued, the hospital expanded, eventually including 150 wards. At the time, it was said to be the largest military medical facility in the world. During the course of the war, some 76,000 patients passed through its wards. For the most part, each ward was a separate one-story building measuring about 30 by 100 feet (9.1 by 31 meters), holding 40 to 60 patients. The wards were organized into five groups, with each group called a hospital and headed by a surgeon. Pember was matron of Hospital Number 2.

The sprawling Chimborazo hospital, located in Richmond, Virginia, opened in 1862 and eventually included 150 wards in 120 buildings. The facility was essentially self-sufficient and included a farm, a natural spring, herds of livestock, and individual buildings for preparing meals, ice, soap, baked goods, storing food, and supplies.

Phoebe Yates Pember's autobiography, *A Southern Woman's Story*, details the hardships she endured as a matron. She writes vivid descriptions of her dank living quarters and the horrible atrocities she saw every day in the hospital room.

At Chimborazo, Pember was the first woman to report for duty as matron. Later, when she wrote about those first days, she titled a chapter "Entry Into Man's Domain."[5] Despite the need for personnel, Pember was not welcomed by most male physicians. Medicine was considered the domain of men, and Pember seemed an intruder. When she arrived for duty, she noticed that "there was no mistaking the stage-whisper which reached my ears from the open door of the office that morning, as the little contract surgeon passed out and informed a friend he met, in a tone of ill-concealed disgust, that *one of them had come.*"[6]

One of the first battles Pember faced was over whiskey. According to Confederate law, matrons were to be in charge of dispensing "spirits," or liquor, to patients. (During the war, doctors commonly prescribed whiskey and other liquors, such as brandy, to the sick and wounded. A typical dose of liquor was two to four ounces.) When Pember sent a requisition for one barrel of whiskey (a one-month supply for her division), the surgeon in charge refused to release it. Pember recalled, "The monthly barrel of whiskey which I was entitled to draw still remained at the dispensary under the guardianship of the apothecary and his clerks, and quarts and pints were issued through any order coming from surgeons or their substitutes, so that the contents were apt to be gone long before I was entitled to draw more, and my sick would suffer for want of the stimulant."[7]

But Pember refused to back down. On her side she had the Confederate law requiring liquors and other luxuries, such as coffee, tea, and milk, to be held and dispensed by the matrons. In her words, "The printed law being at hand for reference, I nailed my colors to the mast, and that evening all the liquor was in my pantry and the key in my pocket."[8]

Through her tenure as matron, Pember faced difficulties of one sort or another involving the whiskey. She was not free of the "onerous" responsibility until federal troops took over the

SLEEPING QUARTERS

As a nurse for the Union army, Louisa May Alcott (1832–1888) served only a few weeks before contracting typhoid. After being sent home, she wrote *Hospital Sketches*, describing army hospital life. In this excerpt, she describes her living quarters:

> For the benefit of any ardent damsel whose patriotic fancy may have surrounded hospital life with a halo of charms, I will briefly describe the bower to which I retired . . . It was well ventilated, for five panes of glass had suffered compound fractures . . . A bare floor supported two iron beds, spread with thin mattresses like plasters . . . A mirror (let us be elegant!) of the dimensions of a muffin, and about as reflective, hung over a tin basin . . . the closet contained a varied collection of bonnets, bottles, bags, boots, bread and butter, boxes and bugs . . . I always opened [the cupboard] with fear and trembling, owing to rats . . .[9]

hospital at war's end. "There were many suspicious circumstances connected with this *institution*," she recalled. "Indeed, if it is necessary to have a hero for this matter-of-fact narrative, the whisky barrel will have to step forward and make his bow."[10]

Another challenge of the new job was cooking. Although Pember's duties included preparing meals for patients, she had little knowledge about the preparation of food. For the first meal, Pember decided to make chicken soup. She ordered two plucked chickens from the steward. Then, as she put it, "For the first time I cut up with averted eyes a raw bird."[11] Finally, the soup was prepared. To Pember's dismay, the first patient to whom she offered the soup tasted it and handed it right back. He said it did not taste like his mother's soup, and he might be willing to eat it "if it war'n't for them *weeds* a-floating round."[12] He was referring to the parsley.

Outside the hospital, Pember worked to adjust to life in a new town. Since no living quarters had been arranged for her, for a time she lived at the hospital, then at the home of the secretary of war. Eventually she rented a room from a woman named Mrs. Skinner. In the evenings, Pember sometimes attended social gatherings, and her sense of fun, intelligence, and good looks made her a welcome guest. According to Thomas Cooper DeLeon, a writer whose topics included the social circuit, Pember was "brisk and brilliant" and had a "pretty, almost Creole accent."[13] Moreover, he said, Pember had "a will of steel under a suave refinement" that served her well in the "fusses"[14] at the hospital.

At Chimborazo, Pember proved herself an exemplary caregiver, tending the physical needs of her patients while acknowledging their fears, dreams, and hopes. She appreciated it when grateful patients wrote poems and slipped them under her office door. She noticed, too, the artistic efforts of those who carved images from wood, bone, or other material. She listened to others tell about the battles they had been in, and she even listened when patients shared recipes from home. She wrote down one soldier's recipe for "sour soup," a concoction of buttermilk and egg-and-cornmeal dumplings, all flavored with "lots of pepper and salt."[15]

As the war wore on, Pember noticed a change in her patients' attitudes. Early in the war, they exhibited devotion to the Confederate cause, fighting what they believed to be an honorable war. She noted, "In no instance up to a certain period did I hear of any remark that savored of personal hatred. They fought for a cause . . . "[16] But late in the war they began to express a deep and personal hatred of the enemy. In part, the shift in view was inspired by the Union army's introduction of black troops, many of whom were former slaves. Even more so, their hatred was motivated by battles at Petersburg, an important rail center 23 miles (37 kilometers)

Despite the harshness of racism that pervaded the war-torn country, African Americans fought with high hopes of ending the conflict. Shown with their band instruments, the members of the 107th U.S. Colored Infantry pose for a group photograph in 1865.

OREGON TRAIL SCHOOL LIBRARY
CASPER, WYOMING

south of Richmond, the Confederate capital. The series of battles that began there in June 1864 would culminate in the defeat of the South the following April.

After the Confederacy's surrender, Pember stayed at Chimborazo, overseeing the care of her patients during the transfer of authority from the South to the North. Finally, she returned to Georgia and published *A Southern Woman's Story* in 1879. She died on March 4, 1913, at the age of eighty-nine.

DR. ESTHER HILL HAWKS

In 1863, on the South Carolina Sea Islands, Dr. Esther Hill Hawks volunteered in the first army hospital for black soldiers. The hospital was not "admitted to the brotherhood of hospitals on quite an even footing," she wrote in her journal. "Favors were a little grudingly bestowed."[1] One of the "annoyances," as she called them, was white soldiers getting bits of scrap iron at a black-smith's shop and throwing them at her patients. Calling the black soldiers names was also a "frequent occurance."[2]

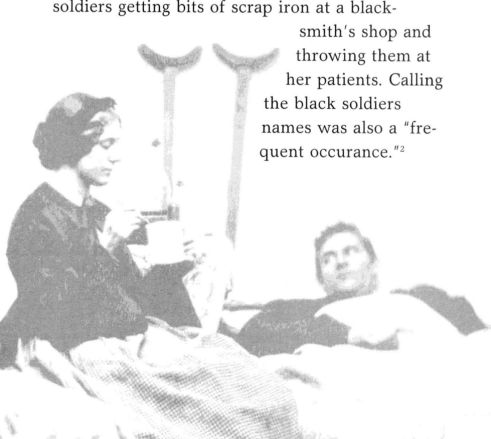

Dr. John Milton Hawks *(left)* advised Esther *(right)* against going into the field of medicine. He felt that his wife's career made their family seem strange and socially unacceptable.

Nevertheless, Hawks remained devoted to her patients, working as a physician and a schoolteacher to black soldiers on the Sea Islands and in Florida until the war's end.

Esther Jane Hill was born on August 4, 1833, in Hookset, New Hampshire, to Parmenas and Jane Kimball Hill. An intelligent child with hazel eyes and black curly hair, she had four older and three younger siblings. After a public school education, she decided, like many women, to teach young people.

In 1854, she married John Milton Hawks, a physician in Manchester, Massachusetts. She began studying Milton's medical books, absorbing the material so quickly that she was soon able to give public lectures on physiology. She then enrolled at the New England Female Medical College in Boston, studying anatomy, surgery, toxicology, and obstetrics. She graduated in 1857, a full-fledged doctor. Hawks's husband, though ostensibly supportive of women's rights, later declared, "I wish Ette [his nickname for Esther] had never seen a medical book, or heard a lecture. It is not a business man-like worker that a husband needs. It is a loving woman."[3]

After the outbreak of war, Hawks went to Washington to obtain a post as an army doctor. To her dismay, the military refused to hire a female physician. Next, she applied to Dorothea Dix, superintendent of army nurses, for a position. Dix rejected her as well, possibly because Hawks did not meet Dix's minimum-age requirement. Not to be deterred, Hawks stayed in Washington until October, volunteering in the hospitals.

Union forces gained control of the Sea Islands off the coast of South Carolina, where they took over cotton plantations and claimed thousands of slaves (abandoned by their masters) as "contraband" of war. In April 1862, Hawks's husband took a job there as a physician, and Hawks followed him in October. She set to work as a teacher to former slaves, observing, "[T]here has been no mental food for them any more than for the swine and cattle with whom their lives are shared . . . they are all eager to go to school . . ."[4] The following month, she extended her classes to include soldiers in the First South Carolina Volunteers, the first official black regiment in the Union army.

Early in March 1863, the regiment marched south to Jacksonville, Florida, leaving behind only the injured and sick. Dr. Milton Hawks was placed in charge of a hospital set up especially for black soldiers. When injured soldiers were brought in from the Jacksonville expedition, Milton welcomed the assistance of his wife. Along with a nurse, Mrs. Strong, they bathed the patients and made up beds with clean sheets. Hawks noted with curiosity that many of the soldiers, who had never slept in clean sheets before, removed them, folded them carefully, and set them aside before sleeping on the bare mattress.

When Milton was sent to accompany "a secret expedition to the coast of Florida," Hawks took charge of the hospital. "Every morning at nine o'clock the disabled are marched down to the hospital in charge of a Sergent and I hold surgens call, for hospital and Regt. [regiment] and with great success."[5] Hawks was in charge of the hospital for three weeks, noting with pleasure that she performed the duties so well that headquarters did not notice it had neglected to appoint an officer to fill in for Milton.

On July 18, news came that 500 wounded men were en route to the hospital. The first group was brought in, 150 soldiers from the Fifty-fourth Massachusetts Infantry, a regiment of black soldiers commanded by Colonel Robert Gould Shaw. At the entrance to Charleston Harbor, they had attacked Fort Wagner, fighting valiantly but finally pulling back when they realized the white troops ordered to support them would not arrive in time. Hawks helped lay them on blankets on the floor, noting the men were "all mangled and ghastly."[6] Many former slaves from town came to their aid with broth, gruel (porridge), fruits, vegetables, cakes, and lemonade. Hawks suspected that they went without food themselves in order to provide for the soldiers. Aid came, too, from the U.S. Sanitary Commission. Hawks wrote, "[N]o one, unless they have had the experience, can imagine the amount of work and worry needed in setting one of these vast military machines [hospitals] in motion!"[7]

Some of the soldiers developed gangrene, and the air inside the hospital stank so badly from

The Sanitary Commission arrives at a fort during the height of the Civil War. Because so many people were dead or injured, the hospitals and clinics became overburdened with work. The Sanitary Commission, which helped clean up the facilities and bury the dead, was always welcomed.

decaying flesh that the afflicted men were moved outdoors. The stench combined with overwork and weakness from a recent fever finally caused Hawks to collapse. At first, she feared she would need to go home to Massachusetts to recuperate, but a week later she returned to work.

Hawks was touched by many sentiments expressed by her patients. One twenty-year-old soldier, Charley Reason, told her, "As soon as the government would take me I came to fight, *not* for

TOTAL RECEIPTS

OF THE

WOMAN'S CENTRAL RELIEF ASSOCIATION,

From May 1st, 1861, to Nov. 1st, 1863.

Flannel Shirts	51,478	Quilts	20,444
Cotton "	117,999	Blankets	6,359
Flannel Drawers	35,284	Sheets	42,760
Cotton "	50,608	Bed Sacks	11,832
Socks	91,576	Pillows	28,096
Slippers	20,255	Pillow Sacks	6,842
Dressing Gowns	12,813	" Cases	57,695
Coats	3,064	Cushions	16,373
Pantaloons	4,122	Towels	98,309
Hdkfs	84,119	Musquito Nets	3,100

Total of Clothing..471,318   **Total of Bedding..291,810**

Lint, bbls	556	Jelly, in jars	16,576
Bandages, bbls	1,047	Wine, in bottles	12,432
Old Cotton, "	466	Cond. Milk, lbs	11,108
Dried Fruit "	1,129	Beef Stock, "	6,043
Vegetables "	278	Groceries, "	16,859
Fresh Fruit " and boxes	128	Pickles, galls	4,470
Fans	10,088	Lemonade, lbs	2,872

By a fair estimate these are valued at

$566,831 14;

In addition to which we have received, in money,

$35,551 38.

The Woman's Central Relief Association required a large amount of clothing, linens, and food to maintain even the most basic standards of health care in their hospitals. A receipt of their expenses, shown above, tallies up all of the costs.

my country, I never had any, but to gain one."[8] Charley, who endured an amputation, died a few hours later. A sergeant from Cincinnati who had attended Oberlin College said, "It isn't that I can't die if necessary; I'm not afraid to die, I came to die fighting for the rights of the black man."[9] Hawks was especially fond of seventeen-year-old Jonny Lott. She asked him, "Jonny, do you ever wish you had been born white?" He said, "I always felt glad to be just what I am, a black boy with no drop of white in me. There is a chance now to do a great deal if one has the heart for it and I am ready to give my other arm, or my life if necessary, for my race!"[10]

Leaving the Sea Islands in November 1863, Hawks accompanied her husband, now promoted to army surgeon, to Hilton Head, South Carolina. Here, as on the Sea Islands, she held classes for black soldiers and volunteered her medical services. A few months later, Milton was transferred to Jacksonville, Florida. Once again, Hawks set up a classroom for the soldiers, teaching when there was time to spare from her work in the hospitals.

Hawks was devoted to her work, but camp life was difficult. She missed having her own medical practice. "I often wonder," she wrote, "if I am doing just as *much* good as I might be in some other sphere—if I am wasting time which should be devoted to my profession."[11] Besides these doubts, other, more private pains intruded. She had been unable to conceive a child. "I have longed for this, prayed for it with all the passionate entreaty of a desolate nature. Why am I denied?"[12] Finally in August, she returned to Massachusetts for rest and recuperation.

Three months later, though, Hawks was back in Hilton Head, teaching school and assisting with medical work, duties she continued until the end of the war. That April, with the Union's victory over the Confederacy, Hawks was overjoyed: "The victory is complete, the surrender unconditional! The army disbanded; soldiers to return home, and all the offices paroled! The city is wild with rejoicing."[13] After the war, Hawks worked as a physician and a teacher, first in Volusia County, Florida, and then in Lynn, Massachusetts. She died at home in Lynn on May 6, 1906.

MARY ANN BICKERDYKE

While some women nurses who served with distinction during the Civil War are notable for their clashes with male physicians and army officers, Mary Ann Bickerdyke achieved remarkable results in organizing medical facilities in the Union armies while garnering the respect of most. Grateful for her service to them, soldiers called her Mother Bickerdyke.

Ironically, Mother Bickerdyke was herself motherless. A native of Knox County, Ohio, she was born to Hiram

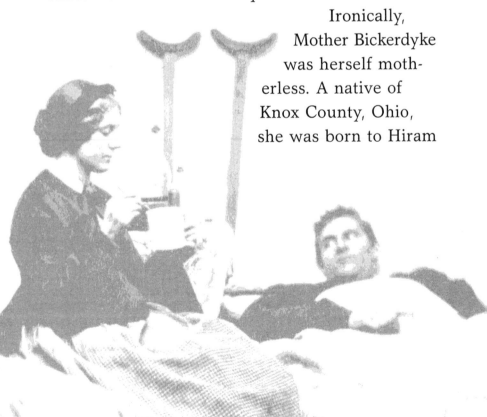

and Annie Ball on July 19, 1817. When she was seventeen months old, her mother died, leaving her in the care of her maternal grandparents, the Rodgerses. After a few years, she was sent to live with other relatives. Thereafter, she moved from one relative's home to another, never finding a place where she truly belonged. A journalist who interviewed Bickerdyke in 1861 reported that she grew up "a servant in the home of strangers."[1] It may be that because Bickerdyke had felt the lack of a mother's nurturing she was able to sense what the soldiers, many of them young, needed in a caregiver.

When questioned about her childhood later in life, Bickerdyke painted a picture of shade trees, streams, and apple orchards. Bickerdyke believed her grandfather's orchard had been planted by none other than Johnny Appleseed. She also recalled the stories of her grandfather Rodgers of his service in the Revolutionary War, including his proud claim that he had been given a pair of wool socks knitted by Martha Washington. These two themes—nature and war—formed the nucleus of Bickerdyke's life, for she became a practitioner of "botanic medicine" and achieved great respect as a nurse in the Civil War.

Little is known of Bickerdyke's youth. A move to Oberlin, Ohio, is likely, but the claim of some historians that she attended Oberlin College and, later, the Physio-Botanic Medical College in Cincinnati are unfounded. Enrollment records at both schools fail to show her matriculation. The confusion over Bickerdyke's formal education—or lack thereof—probably resulted from indignant reactions in Bickerdyke and her friends to accusations that she was uneducated. It seems that her peers began dropping rumors about Oberlin and the medical college to quiet the gossip about her lack of formal education. At any rate, in an interview with a journalist in 1861, at which time the education in question should have been completed, Bickerdyke claimed only to have studied botanic medicine and to have taught herself practical nursing.

In 1847, she married Robert Bickerdyke, a widower with young children. Living in Cincinnati, the couple had three more children. The youngest, a girl named Martha, died when she was two years old, causing Bickerdyke to lament her own lack of medical knowledge. Could she have saved the child, she wondered, if she had studied medicine? When Robert died in 1858 or 1859, she supported her family by practicing botanic medicine. Nature-based, this type of medicine relied on herbs, bark, roots, vegetables, water, and fresh air to treat patients rather than drugs such as opium or treatments such as bloodletting and purgatives.

In 1861, at the Galesburg Congregational Church, Bickerdyke listened as Rev. Edward Beecher read a letter from a doctor stationed with General Ulysses Grant's troops in Illinois. Describing the soldiers' suffering from typhoid

Mary Ann Bickerdyke is pictured in this nineteenth-century engraving, *Midnight on the Battlefield.* Nurses working during the Civil War demonstrated tremendous courage as well as practical skill and were often appreciated for their unending compassion toward wounded or dying soldiers.

fever, and dysentery, the doctor pleaded for help. The congregation raised $500, and Bickerdyke volunteered to deliver the gift. Within a mile of the camp in Cairo, Illinois, she could smell a stench in the air. Once in camp, she saw piles of amputated limbs, dead dogs, and garbage.

After taking in the filthy, noxious situation, Bickerdyke rolled up her sleeves and went to work. She boiled uniforms and linens, all filthy and crusted with blood. She bathed the sick and wounded, wiping away battlefield grime and making sure each had clean clothes and fresh straw in his bed. With supplies she had brought, she cooked chicken dinners for everyone. Her whirlwind of activity inspired the nickname Cyclone in Calico.

The Cyclone in Calico kept going. After arranging for the care of her children back home, she turned her attention to the soldiers. She continued to treat patients at the military hospital in Cairo, often assisted by Mary Safford, a young woman who later became a physician. Although the doctor in charge of the hospital protested Bickerdyke's presence, General Grant ordered that she be allowed to stay, appointing her matron.

By 1862, Bickerdyke had joined the U.S. Sanitary Commission. After doing a series of fundraising speeches for Mary Livermore's branch of the

ANESTHESIA

In both Union and Confederate hospitals, soldiers undergoing major surgery, such as the amputation of a limb, were sometimes given chloroform as an anesthetic when it was available. A liquid distilled from chloride of lime and alcohol, chloroform was applied to a small cloth that was then shaped into a cone and held like a tent just over the patient's nose and mouth. After initial sobs and groans, the patient fell into unconsciousness. If, during the operation, the patient had trouble breathing and death seemed close, the chloroform-soaked cloth was removed in order to administer cold air, cold water, an enema, and, if available, electricity. After the operation, pain was sometimes managed with combinations of opium, laudanum (an opium derivative), and whiskey, depending on what was available.

An amputation is performed in a hospital tent at the Battle of Gettysburg, in 1863. At the time, painful operations such as amputations were usually performed without the benefit of anesthesia.

commission, Bickerdyke received a thank-you gift of a magnificent labor-saving device, a washing machine, for her hospital. In a speech delivered in Milwaukee, she asked her listeners, "Suppose, gentlemen, you had got to give to-night one thousand dollars or your right leg, would it take long to decide which to surrender? . . . I have got eighteen hundred boys in my hospital . . . who have given one arm, and one leg, and some have given both . . ."[2]

With her dedication to the care and comfort of common soldiers, not the officers and surgeons, Bickerdyke truly embodied her nickname of "Mother." Dr. L. P. Brocket, describing Bickerdyke in 1867, wrote, "She devoted her attention almost exclusively to the care of the private soldiers; the officers, she said, had enough to look after them; but it was the men, poor fellows, with but a private's pay, a private's fare, and a private's dangers, to whom she was particularly called. They were dear to somebody, and she would be a mother to them."[3] By all accounts, Mother Bickerdyke was dear to these soldiers.

On one occasion, when she caught a ward master wearing clothing and slippers that should have gone to patients, she ordered him to remove the stolen articles immediately. As patients looked on, he stripped down to his underwear and gave the clothing back. Dr. Brocket declared, "For her 'boys,' she would brave everything; if the surgeons or attendants at the hospitals were unfaithful, she denounced them with a terrible vehemence, and always managed to secure their dismission; if the Government officers were slow or delinquent in forwarding needed supplies, they were sure to be reported at headquarters by her . . ."[4] Through it all, as historians are fond of noting, when Bickerdyke faced resistance from a doctor or officer, she declared, "My authority comes from God. Do you have anyone ranking higher than that?"[5]

While soldiers regarded Mother Bickerdyke with respect, admiration, and affection, some of the surgeons and officers did not.

A photograph of Mary Ann Bickerdyke in her old age. Bickerdyke's strong-willed manner intimidated others and helped her achieve great reforms in medical care.

Bickerdyke challenged their authority by doing things her way, whether or not they agreed. And if one of them performed his duties carelessly or dishonestly, she reprimanded him for it. On one occasion, a surgeon, angry with Bickerdyke for accusing him of misconduct, complained to General Grant. Though Grant responded with humor, he meant every word he said: "Mother Bickerdyke outranks everybody, even [President] Lincoln. If you have run amuck of her I advise you to get out quickly before she has you under arrest."[6] On another occasion, when Bickerdyke caused a drunken surgeon to be dismissed, he went to General William T. Sherman to be reinstated. Sherman refused, saying, "I can do nothing for you. She [out]ranks me."[7]

After Cairo, Mother Bickerdyke worked on the hospital transport ship City of Memphis on five trips as it carried wounded Union soldiers to Fort Donelson in northwestern Tennessee. She visited hospitals in Illinois and still others in St. Louis and Louisville. There she joined efforts with nurses hired by Dorothea Dix, superintendent of women nurses for the Union army, as well as Catholic sisters who had volunteered. Then Bickerdyke moved on with Grant's troops down the Mississippi, setting up field hospitals as needed. In all, she set up

This drawing (top) shows the hospital boat named Red Rover as it floats down the Mississippi River. The drawings of the inside of the boat depict a nurse (middle) and the sick ward (bottom).

about 300 field hospitals, working with agents of the Sanitary Commission. She treated the wounded in nineteen battles.

One night following a battle, Colonel John A. Logan happened to notice a shrouded figure inspecting the lifeless bodies on the battlefield. Thinking the person might be one of those who robbed the dead, he sent an orderly to bring the intruder to him. The person turned out to be Bickerdyke, who had been searching for overlooked wounded. She declared, "Some soldiers in the frozen mud may be still alive. Do you expect me to sleep?"[8]

With earnestness and zeal and despite growing exhaustion, Bickerdyke worked through the end of the war. After the conflict, she received a continual flow of thanks from soldiers who claimed she had saved their lives. Until her death on November 8, 1901, she occupied her time with one philanthropic cause after another, including the Chicago Home for the Friendless, a veterans' boarding house in Kansas, and the Salvation Army. She also worked for a time at the U.S. Mint—a job she got with the help of her friend John A. Logan, who had become a California senator, who had watched her search for wounded on that dark battlefield.

CLARA BARTON

5

At Antietam Creek, near Sharpsburg, Maryland, more than 80,000 soldiers clashed in battle. It was September 17, 1861. Northerners and Southerners alike were beginning to realize just how bloody the war between the states would be. Near the battlefield, Clara Barton pulled a wagonload of medical supplies, food, lanterns, and other necessities into the yard of a farmhouse. Already the ground was covered with several hundred injured soldiers. As she bent to give water to one of

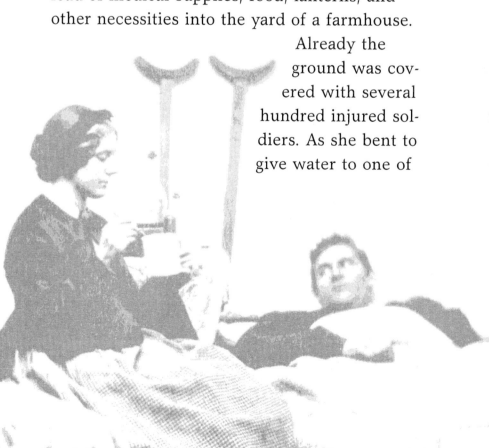

the wounded, a bullet ripped through her sleeve and struck the soldier, killing him. "I have never mended that hole in my sleeve," Barton recalled. "I wonder if a soldier ever does mend a bullet hole in his coat?"[1]

Born on Christmas Day, 1821, Clarissa Harlow Barton was the youngest of five children in a farming family in Oxford, Massachusetts. Her father, Stephen Barton, had been a soldier under General "Mad Anthony" Wayne in the Indian Wars. He often entertained young Clara with tales of his war days, acting out imaginary battles with her. She dreamed of becoming a soldier herself. Clara's mother, Sarah Stone Barton, was a hard-working, thrifty, outspoken woman. She signed antislavery petitions and, in Clara's words, "always did two days' work in one."[2]

To Clara, her siblings, who were ten to seventeen years older, seemed like four additional parents. "All took charge of me," she recalled, "all educated me, each according to [his or her own] personal taste."[3] From Stephen she learned math, and from David she learned "boy's" skills, including horseback riding, tying square knots, and throwing balls. Having learned to read by age three, she was attending school by age four. With Sally, who later became a teacher, she read literature and poetry. In this spirited family, Clara grew up shy, a personality trait she battled all her life.

At age eleven, when Clara got her first taste of nursing, she discovered the work to be fulfilling. When David fell from a barn roof and was badly injured, she cared for him and administered his medications. Later, when smallpox swept through the area, she nursed local victims.

At age seventeen, she began teaching school in a one-room schoolhouse and continued to teach for nearly fifteen years. But in 1853, after being passed over as principal of a school she herself had started, she left teaching, frustrated that women, no matter how qualified, were denied positions of authority.

At the outbreak of the Civil War, Barton was working as a copyist in the U.S. Patent Office in Washington, the Union capital. She was thirty-nine years old, unmarried (not for lack of suitors, but by choice), and a staunch supporter of the Union. When she heard that soldiers in a Union regiment had been injured in Baltimore and would soon arrive by train in Washington, she rushed to the station. With a few other women, she wrapped their wounds with handkerchiefs.

Before founding the Red Cross, Clara Barton worked at the U.S. Patent Office and gathered food and supplies for the Union army. This photograph shows her in 1862.

Baltimore, she learned, was a city of mixed loyalties, with some citizens supporting the South and others supporting the North. The march of the Union regiment across the city to catch the train to Washington had attracted Confederate sympathizers, who taunted the troops and began flinging stones.

The soldiers fought back, shots were fired, and a riot ensued, ending in the deaths of four soldiers and twelve civilians. In response to the event, Barton wrote, "[T]he darkest page in our country's history is now being written in lines of blood!"[4]

She learned that many of the soldiers had lost their baggage in Baltimore. They had the clothes on their backs, but nothing more. Right away she went through the closets and pantries of her own house, gathering food and sewing supplies. Next she went to the merchants in town, persuading them to open on a Sunday so she could fill large wicker baskets with soap, food, and other items for the soldiers.

That spring and summer, Barton watched as thousands of troops poured into the city, setting up camp wherever there was space. Facilities such as the Treasury Department, the Navy Yard, and warehouses became makeshift campsites. One regiment set out bedrolls in the Patent Office where Barton worked. She went from place to place, nursing the sick and injured and delivering supplies. She placed an advertisement in the *Worcester Spy*, her hometown newspaper, inviting people to send bandages, salves, canned fruit, pickled vegetables, clothing, and other items for the soldiers. Within a few months, she filled her house and three warehouses with donations.

Talking to the soldiers, Barton learned of the horrifying conditions an injured or ill soldier faced at the battlefront. In *Clara Barton: Healing the Wounds*, Cathy East Dubowski wrote, "Medicine, food, and clothing were carried to the front in slow-moving horse-drawn wagons that often took

Horse-drawn carts like this "Rucker ambulance" were used to transport the sick from the battlefields to the hospitals during the Civil War. Rucker ambulances could carry wounded in both a sitting and lying position. All the same, riding in bouncing wagons over uneven ground was often a severe ordeal for the sick and injured.

days to catch up with the army. Overworked surgeons treated only the most serious cases. Wounds became infected as soldiers lay on the ground waiting for help. Many bled to death in rough wagon rides back to the hospitals."[5] After learning of these conditions, Barton requested permission from the War Department to take supplies directly to the front lines. At first it was difficult to persuade authorities to allow a woman near the fighting. But finally she obtained a pass.

With her pass, Barton traveled from battle to battle with horse-drawn wagons loaded with medical supplies and food. She nursed soldiers by the dozen when they were carried away from battle. As she worked, shots sometimes split the air overhead. In some instances, the injured had to be hauled away quickly because as the battle moved closer, it overtook the grounds where wounded lay. In these instances, Barton stayed with her patients until the last possible moment. During these last-minute evacuations, her ability to ride a horse proved to be a life-saving skill.

On August 9, she heard about a battle at Cedar Mountain in Virginia. Stonewall Jackson had led 25,000 Confederate troops to victory over Union troops under John Pope. Three hundred fourteen Union soldiers had died in the battle, and 1,465 were wounded. More than 600 others were missing. When Barton arrived at Cedar Mountain four days later, she supplied surgeons with fresh dressings, provided soldiers with clean clothing, and prepared and served soup. All the while, shells burst in the background.

From Cedar Mountain, Barton traveled by wagon to the Second Battle of Bull Run (known in the South as the Second Battle of Manassas). Wounded soldiers lay on hay that had been spread

Clara Barton is shown here raising the American flag in a cemetery that was once the site of a prison. This sketch was printed in *Harper's Weekly* right after the end of the Civil War. Barton's mission of finding lost soldiers gave their families comfort and hope.

on the ground, and wagon upon wagon brought scores of additional injured. Soon they lay so close together that Barton feared treading upon an arm or leg as she moved among them. After dark, she feared that the accidental dropping of a candle would set the whole scene afire. She and other volunteers worked into the night, dressing wounds and distributing food and water. In a letter, she wrote with her characteristic trace of wit that they had "three thousand guests to serve."[6] Beyond them, the battle raged on. As the enemy pushed closer, wagons began transporting the injured away. Barton refused to leave until the last of the wounded had been carried away. Sixteen thousand Union soldiers died in the battle.

From the Second Battle of Bull Run, Barton traveled to a battlefield in Chantilly, Virginia. Then she headed to Antietam Creek, where, on September 17, the bloody Battle of Antietam was fought. As her brave service became known among Union soldiers, they began calling her the Angel of the Battlefield. Until the end of the war, she distributed supplies and worked as a battle-field nurse. Barton continually risked her life by nursing men at the front, saving countless lives.

After the war, she gave lectures on her wartime work, raising awareness for the vital

SUSIE KING TAYLOR

Susie King Taylor (1848–1912) was not an average wartime nurse. She was an African

Susie King Taylor

American teenager, born a slave. Early in the war, during a Union attack on Fort Pulaski in Georgia, Taylor fled with nine relatives to the Union side and was taken in as "contraband" of war. When African American men formed a volunteer infantry regiment (later known as the Thirty-third United States Colored Troops, or USCT), fourteen-year-old Taylor joined them as laundress and nurse. Often she tended the injured while artillery shells whizzed overhead. In July 1863, while on temporary duty with the Fifty-fourth Massachusetts Infantry, Taylor assisted Clara Barton, nursing the wounded after the Fifty-fourth's attack on Fort Wagner in South Carolina. She remained Barton's assistant for eight months before returning to the USCT.

At left, some pages from Clara Barton's lecture about her service in the Civil War. Barton was already a skilled lecturer before the war, as she had spent several years as a teacher in various schools before finally opening her own.

service of trained medical personnel during war. After working for the International Red Cross, she founded the American Red Cross in 1881. After a short retirement in Glen Echo, New York, Barton died on April 12, 1912.

DR. MARY EDWARDS WALKER

6

Mary Edwards Walker holds the distinction of being the only woman surgeon known to have received an official appointment during the Civil War. Moreover, she is the only woman ever to have received the Congressional Medal of Honor, the United States's highest military award. Signed by President Andrew Johnson, her citation declares that she "has devoted herself with much patriotic zeal to the sick and wounded soldiers, both in the field and hospitals" and that she "also endured hardships as a prisoner of war four months in a Southern prison."[1]

The fifth of six children, Mary Edwards Walker was born on November 26, 1832, to Alvah and Vesta Walker. Along with her siblings, Mary grew up doing chores on the 33-acre (13-hectare) family farm in Oswego Town, New York. At a local school where her parents taught, she received her formal education. At home, her parents encouraged her to read widely, and she devoured her father's medical texts. She decided she would become a doctor.

At the age of twenty-one, Walker enrolled in Syracuse Medical College in New York. Her course of study included anatomy, obstetrics, surgery, and chemistry. In those days, a student earned a medical degree in two years, and Walker graduated in 1855. She was now Dr. Mary Walker. Soon after graduation she married Dr. Albert Miller, a former classmate. The marriage, however, was unsuccessful. After many years of separation, Walker obtained a divorce in 1869. She never remarried, nor did she have children.

When the Civil War started, Walker knew she wanted to serve the Union as a military doctor. She went to Washington and applied for a commission.

While waiting for a response to her application, she volunteered in a makeshift hospital in the U.S. Patent Office—the same office where Clara Barton worked. After learning that the army had denied her a commission, Walker stayed on as a volunteer. But true to form, she did not quit her quest to serve officially. She applied again, this time to the U.S. surgeon general, Clement A. Finley. He also rejected her. It seemed no one with authority believed a woman could—or should—work as an army doctor.

For a time, Walker shifted her energies to the wounded pouring into Washington. She worked with confidence and authority. On one occasion, she went to a prison for deserters, concerned for their health, and she demanded entrance by saying, "I am Dr. Walker of the Union Army. I command you to let me pass."

Not long before, Secretary of War Edwin Stanton had appointed Dorothea Dix as superintendent of female nurses. On at least one occasion, Walker and Dix worked in the same hospital ward. Although Walker admired Dix's earlier work on behalf of the mentally ill, she had little patience for what she called Dix's "sham modesty"[2] when it came to bedridden soldiers. A patient's foot sticking out of the bedclothes was indecent enough to cause Dix to turn her head. In contrast, Walker matter-of-factly walked up and tucked the foot back in.

Hoping additional training would help get her a military commission, Walker attended the Hygeia Therapeutic College in New York City in 1862. Perhaps the most groundbreaking idea she studied there was that keeping patients' wounds

This photograph of Armory Square Hospital in Washington, D.C., shows the close quarters and the limited space in many hospitals during the Civil War.

GERMS: THE UNSEEN ENEMY

On Civil War battlefields, a soldier faced death not only from attack by the enemy but also from attack by microscopic germs. In fact, two-thirds of all soldiers' deaths in the Civil War did not come from battlefield wounds but from infectious diseases. Dysentery as well as diarrhea killed more soldiers than wounds caused from battlefield fighting. C. Keith Wilbur, MD, writes, "Since surgeons had no knowledge of the germ theory, sterile operating conditions would have made no sense. A slosh of water was good enough to clear a bloody operating table, the same old sponges and rinse water would wash the wound, and the contaminated hands and instruments would add more germs to a site that needed no further insult. If all went well, 'laudable' pus would be evidence of normal healing. . ."[3]

clean could save lives. At this time, the dangers germs posed to wounds were poorly understood. Doctors did not sterilize operating tools, tables, or water used to clean wounds. Many patients who died could have survived if they had only been treated hygienically.

Late in 1862, Walker returned to her volunteer work, this time in Warrenton, Virginia, where there was an outbreak of typhoid fever. Though she had not received an army commission, from this point forward she dressed in an officer's blue uniform of gold-striped pants, felt hat with gold braid, and a green surgeon's sash. In her quest for a commission, she wrote directly to President Lincoln. She described herself as a woman with "energy, enthusiasm, professional abilities and patriotism"[4] and said her strongest desire was to serve her country in a battlefield assignment. Lincoln's reply was speedy, but disappointing. He would not help her.

Over the next year, Walker traveled to Falmouth and then to Chattanooga at the front lines. Twelve miles (19 km) away, in Chickamauga, Georgia, 120,000 soldiers clashed at the bloody Battle of Chickamauga Creek. After two days (September 19–20, 1863), casualties were immense, with 16,000 Union soldiers and 18,000 Confederate soldiers dead, wounded, or missing. Tens of thousands of wounded Union soldiers poured into Chattanooga, where Walker had just arrived. Eager to help, she worked at Gordon's Mill, southeast of Chattanooga. Here, Walker's energy and effectiveness impressed both Major General Alexander McCook and Major General George H. Thomas, the "Rock of Chickamauga." Both officers upheld their support of her when the medical director of the Army of the Cumberland, Dr. Perin, attempted to send Walker away. With McCook's and Thomas's support, she held her post.

During late 1863 and early 1864, besides doctoring soldiers at Gordon's Mill, Walker carried medical supplies to desperate civilians in the surrounding region. With Confederate troops in the area, Walker's forays behind enemy lines were risky, especially since she wore her army uniform. On April 10, 1864, the inevitable happened. Confederate soldiers captured her.

After a stop at a nearby Confederate camp where she treated soldiers, Walker was taken to a Richmond prison. Here, the trousers-clad woman doctor attracted curiosity and loathing. Captain Joseph Semmes reacted with venom. In a letter to his wife, he wrote that he and everyone else was "amused" and "disgusted" to see Walker in her Union uniform, and he called her "a thing that nothing but the debased and the depraved Yankee nation could produce—a female doctor." In a scathing conclusion, he declared, "I was in hopes that the General [Joseph E. Johnston] would have had her . . . put in a lunatic asylum."[5]

Considering the horrid conditions of mental institutions of the day, Walker's prison may just as well have been an asylum. Rats skittered across the floor, insects crawled on her mattress, and the food was so poor that malnutrition caused a rapid decay in her eyesight.

Four months later, Walker was exchanged, along with other Union prisoners, for Confederate prisoners. To her surprise, the Union army then paid her $432.36 in salary for her service between March and August 1864. To Walker, who had before worked as a volunteer,

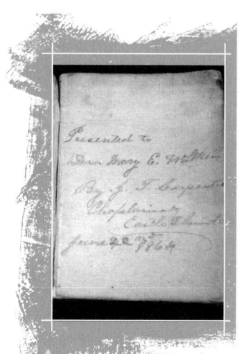

After being captured by Confederates, Mary Edwards Walker was kept in a prison in Richmond, Virginia. Reverend T. J. Carpenter, a Confederate chaplain, gave her this pocket-sized Bible while she remained a prisoner of war.

A field hospital in Virginia after a devastating battle on June 27, 1862. With the number of wounded soldiers, makeshift hospitals such as this one were always in need of medical professionals.

the paycheck was an affirmation that she had found a legitimate place in the army. Her pleasure deepened when, a few weeks later, she was appointed acting assistant surgeon for the United States Army, with a salary of $100 a month. The position was that of a contract surgeon, so she was still a civilian, but the appointment confirmed her legitimacy to practice.

During the remaining eight months of the war, Walker's assignments took her first to a women's prison hospital in Louisville, Kentucky, and then to an orphanage in Clarksville, Tennessee, where she treated children and war refugees. Although her desire was to serve in field hospitals, she applied herself to her assignments.

A few months after the war ended, Walker

Perhaps one of the first innovators to introduce pants into the female wardrobe, Walker is shown here in a man's suit and her Medal of Honor.

was awarded the Medal of Honor for her service during the war. Awarded for the first time, the Medal of Honor was for those who "most distinguish themselves by their gallantry in action, and other soldier-like qualities."[6] There was no doubt that Walker had demonstrated soldier-like qualities, but she had never fought in battle—the "action" named in the wording of the medal's purpose. Still, President Andrew Johnson, who signed her citation himself, supported Walker's candidacy.

Until the end of her life, Walker wore her Medal of Honor. Even after the medal was revoked, along with 910 others, in 1917, after a redefining of qualifications, she wore her medal defiantly. It was just as well, for sixty years later, in 1977, Secretary of the Army Clifford Alexander restored the honor to her posthumously. As of 2003, Mary Edwards Walker remained the only woman to have received the Medal of Honor.

SALLY L. TOMPKINS

7

Sally L. Tompkins, one of the most effectual Civil War nurses, established a private hospital for Confederate soldiers in Richmond, Virginia, in 1861. Of all the army medical facilities, hers had the highest survival rate. Of 1,333 patients under her care, only 73 died. Her establishment and administration of an effective hospital is remarkable in light of the fact that the South had no formal organization for civilian nurses and volunteers, unlike the North, which relied on the U.S. Sanitary

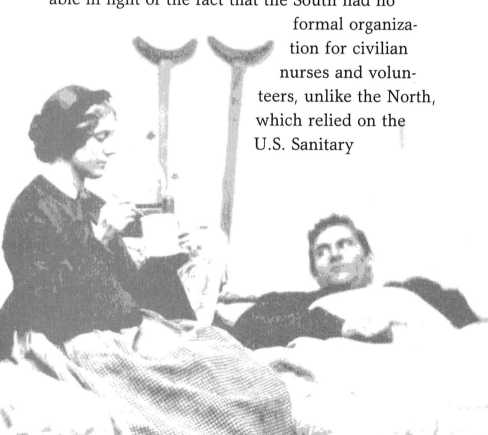

BATTLE OF BULL RUN VA JULY 21ST 1861.
Gallant charge of the Zouaves and defeat of the rebel Black Horse Cavalry

The Battle of Bull Run was the first major land battle in the Civil War. Over four thousand people lost their lives, and hundreds more were wounded. The battle was catastrophic, as the Confederates soon learned that their army was unorganized. Many of their soldiers were old men or young boys with no military training.

Commission. At a time when medicine was a man's domain, Tompkins did what she believed to be expedient, even crucial, using her own finances and willpower.

A native of Poplar Grove, Virginia, Sally Louisa Tompkins was born on November 9, 1833. A child of wealthy parents, her needs were generously provided for, even after her father's death. She and her mother moved to Richmond, where they lived on the inheritance left by Mr.

Tompkins. After the U.S. Civil War erupted in April 1861, twenty-seven-year-old Tompkins decided to use her inheritance to support the Confederate war effort. In Richmond, which soon became the Confederate capital, she opened Robertson Hospital to treat injured and ill Confederate soldiers.

Tompkins established Robertson Hospital after one of the war's early conflicts, the First Battle of Bull Run, fought on July 21, 1861. On this summer day, about 37,000 Union soldiers marched toward Richmond with an eye to take the city. On both sides, military leaders expected the war to end quickly, failing to anticipate how it would escalate. On that July day, civilian spectators accompanied the Union army, set up picnics, and sat back to watch the North trounce the South. But events played out differently than they expected.

The Union's advance toward Richmond was blocked by General P. G. T. Beauregard and his 22,000 Confederate soldiers. Joined later by 10,000 additional Confederates led by General Joseph E. Johnston, the Southern army routed the Northerners. Union soldiers and spectators alike retreated. Between 1,700 and 2,000 Confederate men were wounded or dead, and the injured poured into Richmond.

This home in Manassas, Virginia, known as Stone House, was converted to a military hospital during the Civil War. Many families offered their private residences for use during the conflict, and wounded soldiers often found themselves recovering in makeshift hospitals that were actually schools, churches, or other public institutions.

In Richmond, Tompkins leapt to meet the need for medical care. She saw that all available hospitals were overflowing, and soldiers were being nursed in private homes. A more organized and sanitary system of caring for the wounded would raise the injured soldiers' chances of survival. To this end, Tompkins appealed to a Richmond judge, John Robertson, for use of his large house. With his approval, she converted the house into a hospital, calling the facility Robertson

Hospital. Besides herself and four slaves, volunteers helped care for its wounded.

While women nurses cared for injured on both sides of the war, they were at first discouraged. Although women had been nursing family members and the occasional neighbor as a matter of course, traditional values hindered women from providing the same care to strangers, especially to men. People believed that the bloody gore of wartime injuries, including amputations, head wounds, stomach wounds, and the like, were too horrific for women to face. It was more appropriate, they thought, if women stuck close to home, sewing and knitting clothing for the soldiers, collecting supplies and donations, and providing similar "womanly" services.

A photograph of the medically talented, "Captain" Sally Tompkins. Tompkins's gifts for healing the sick made her hospital the first choice for the severely wounded, people who might have been considered hopeless by other hospitals.

Tompkins's heroic work did not escape the notice of powerful figures in the Confederate government, and her success at running an effective and self-funded facility probably saved her enterprise. Three months after she opened the hospital, Confederate president Jefferson Davis ordered all private hospitals for soldiers closed or placed under military control. Some of these medical facilities, which charged for their services, were providing inadequate care. Others were keeping in bed soldiers who army officials believed should already be back on duty. Tompkins was determined to keep her hospital under her own control.

She requested and was granted a meeting with President Davis, at which she asked that control of Robertson Hospital remain in her hands. Historians have speculated that President Davis agreed to her plan because she funded the hospital herself, while others point out the amazing survival rate that must already have been evident. At any rate, Davis devised an ingenious plan for allowing Robertson Hospital to remain under Tompkins's control. He commissioned Tompkins as a captain of cavalry in the Confederate army. As a result, she could keep her hospital open and operate it with the cooperation of the military. Of all the women who

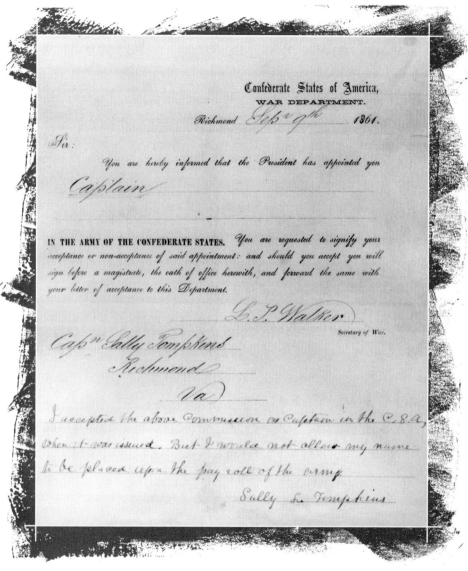

The signature of Sally L. Tompkins can be seen on this document from Confederate Secretary of War L. P. Walker, who commissioned her medical services as an official captain beginning on September 9, 1861. Thanks to the influence of Confederate president Jefferson Davis, Tompkins remained in control of Robertson Hospital throughout the Civil War.

served the Confederate cause, Tompkins was the only one commissioned in the army.

Although located in Virginia, Robertson Hospital received wounded soldiers from across the South. This was no time for loyalties based on a particular state, but rather a time for all Southerners to unite. When Mary Boykin Chesnut, a volunteer, asked Tompkins whether there were any patients from the Carolinas in the hospital to visit and offer gifts to, Tompkins set her straight. All soldiers were to be treated with equal devotion. She told Chesnut, "I never ask where the sick and wounded come from."[1]

As superintendent of the hospital, one of Tompkins's duties was to manage the preparation and distribution of food to patients. These duties fell to matrons, or head nurses, in army hospitals. For example, at the Union Hospital in Alexandria, Virginia, Jane Stuart Woolsey (1830–1891) was superintendent of nurses and managed six different "special diets" for patients: the roast beef and pudding diet, the eggs and milk diet, the vegetable diet, the milk porridge diet, the beef tea diet, and the gruel diet. While monitoring the cooking, the matron made sure the correct items were included in each meal, including sweets as were allotted. As Woolsey wrote in *Hospital Days*, the superintendent of nurses "was expected to follow the food from the commissary storehouse down the sick man's throat."[2]

Over the course of the war, Tompkins remained a solid fixture at her hospital in Richmond, earning the respect of those around her. Writing in 1907 in *Belles, Beaux, and Brains of the* [18]*60s*, Thomas Cooper DeLeon described her as "original, old-fashioned and tireless in welldoing." He wrote that she was "as resolute as a veteran"[3] in her service to the Confederacy.

Affectionately known as Captain Sally, Tompkins operated her hospital for the duration of the war using her own money, supplemented with government rations. In June 1865, two months after the war ended, Tompkins closed the doors of Robertson Hospital. Upon her death on July 25, 1916, in Richmond, Virginia, she was buried with military honors.

KATE CUMMING

8

Kate Cumming, one of the most devoted nurses of the Civil War, was not born an American citizen. Born in Edinburgh, Scotland, in 1835, she moved as a child with her family to Mobile, Alabama. In her mid-twenties and unmarried when the war broke out, she heard Reverend Benjamin M. Miller's call for women to volunteer as nurses at the front. At first, since her family disapproved, she only collected blankets and supplies for Confederate troops. But when she saw a regiment of soldiers leaving for war, many

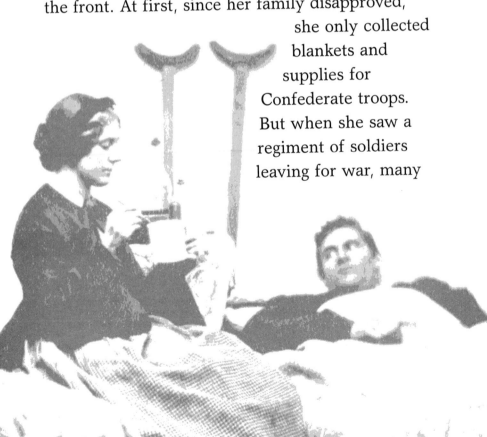

of them her childhood companions, she decided that she must volunteer as a nurse. Her father finally gave his support, but her brothers-in-law asserted that "nursing soldiers was no work for a refined lady."[1]

Along with about forty women, Cumming left Mobile on April 7, 1862, traveling by train toward Corinth, Mississippi. The next day they disembarked in Okolona, Mississippi, about 60 miles (97 km) from their destination, to wait for a permit to enter Corinth. It had rained heavily, the weather was dreary, and the women were dismayed to find that there were no available hotel rooms. Hearing of their plight, local families took the nurses in, and Cumming and a few others went to the home of Mrs. Haughton. One of their hostess's granddaughters described the reception they were likely to receive from the doctors in the army hospitals. Cumming wrote in her journal, "It seems that the surgeons entertain great prejudice against admitting ladies into the hospital in the capacity of nurses. The surgeon in charge, Dr. Caldwell, has carried this so far that he will not even allow the ladies of the place to visit patients."[2]

On April 11, she arrived in Corinth, finally feeling as though she were "in the *service* in reality."[3]

The Tishomingo Hotel in Corinth, Mississippi, is pictured in this 1861 photograph. The Tishomingo was converted to a Confederate hospital after the Battle of Shiloh. When Corinth was lost to invading Union forces, Confederate soldiers retaliated by burning the structure to the ground. The Tishomingo had also been used as a train station and was called the Crossroads of the Confederacy before its demise.

Cumming was nervous. Although she had never been near a large army or seen an injured man, she was about to see plenty of both. Upon arrival at the Tishomingo Hotel, which had been converted into a hospital, she was struck by its filth, gore, and tragedy. If she had harbored any romantic ideas about wartime nursing, those were dashed. "None of the glories of the war were presented here,"[4] she wrote. The reality of the conflict was overwhelming. "Nothing that I had ever heard or read had given me the faintest idea of the horrors witnessed here," she wrote. "I do not think that words are in our vocabulary expressive enough to present to the mind the realities of that sad scene."[5] She saw wounded soldiers—Confederate and Union (also called "Federals")—lying "so close together that it was almost impossible to walk without stepping on them."[6] Her first tasks were to bathe patients and give them water to drink. She noted, "If I were to live a hundred years, I should never forget the poor sufferers' gratitude; for every little thing, done for them."[7]

She was struck by the immensity of the suffering and the task ahead of her. "The foul air from this mass of

A photograph of Kate Cumming taken after the war. Her journal describes the nursing experience as a social rather than medical one. She believed that the sick and wounded needed more than just physical attention; they also needed kindness to get well.

human beings at first made me giddy and sick, but I soon got over it. We have to walk, and when we give the men any thing, kneel, in blood and water; but we think nothing of it at all."[8]

Cumming worked about two months at the Tishomingo Hotel before her group was transferred. On her last day there, she wrote, "We have seen many sad sights and much suffering since we came to this place; still, I shall ever look back on these two months with sincere gratification, and feel that I have lived for something."[9] In Okolona once again, she waited to see in which direction the army would move. In two months' time, the town had become swamped with wounded soldiers and refugees. She spent her days nursing them in private homes, hospitals, tents, and at the railway station as cars full of wounded arrived. She sewed clothing for the soldiers, worrying about the quality of care they received. She wrote, "I hear many complaints about the bad treatment our men are receiving in the hospitals. I have been told that many a day they get only one meal, and that of badly-made soup, and as badly-made bread."[10]

After a ten-week visit to Mobile, Cumming traveled in earnest, working as a nurse in each city where she stopped. By the end of 1862, she had gone to Chattanooga, Tennessee, and Dalton, Georgia. From 1863 through the end of the war, she traveled throughout Georgia, Alabama, and Tennessee. At times, she helped move the wounded away from the advance of the enemy. On July 1, 1863, she wrote, "News has come that the enemy is across the river, and intends shelling the place. We are having hospital flags put up, but I do not see that they will do any good, as it is said the enemy pay no respect to them. We are packing up in a hurry to move. Our hospital being near the river, we will be *honored* by the first shot."[11]

During her travels, she kept a journal. While early entries describe the newness of nursing and war and soldiers, her thoughts gradually turned to the political leaders' strategies, her hopes for the war's outcome, her worry for the soldiers, and her sorrow each time a patient died.

A subject that caused her particular distress was the refusal of many women to nurse soldiers—or even to enter the hospitals—on the grounds that such actions were unladylike, even immodest. Public opinion held that a hospital was no place for a respectable woman. Cumming noted, "Scarcely a day passes that I do not hear some

Pictured above is the monument to the Sisters of Mercy for their efforts during the Civil War. The monument is in Washington, D.C., and portrays twelve nuns who represent the different orders who nursed soldiers and provided aid during the war.

derogatory remarks about the ladies who are working in the hospitals." In her journal on December 8, 1863, she poured out her frustration and outrage. "I am thoroughly disgusted with this kind of talk."[12] She found it ironic that hundreds of sisters of the Roman Catholic Church deemed it honorable to nurse soldiers, while other women who considered themselves Christian thought the same actions to be wrong. Cumming concluded that "in truth, none but the 'refined

SISTERS OF THE BATTLEFIELD

During the Civil War, more than 600 sisters of the Roman Catholic Church volunteered to nurse injured Union and Confederate soldiers. Working in different geographical regions, they tended the wounded in mobile hospitals, on hospital transport ships, and in military hospitals set up in convents, schools, hospitals, tents, and private homes. When Union soldiers marched on Vicksburg, Mississippi, the Confederate army retreated into Alabama, and the Sisters of Mercy accompanied them to provide medical care. On the waterways, five Sisters of the Poor of St. Francis sailed on the *Superior*, a steamer towing barges full of soldiers, and other sisters nursed soldiers on the *Red Rover*, the *Commodore*, the *Whillden*, and other boats. In 1862, after Union troops seized General Robert E. Lee's home in Virginia, sixty Daughters of Charity set up a medical facility in the house.

---

and modest' have any business in hospitals"[13]— implying that those who refused to help the sick and wounded were the unladylike ones.

Despite the continual loss of lives, Cumming tried to remain upbeat and optimistic. Weeks before the war ended, she wrote,

We seem to be completely hemmed in on all sides. I hear that the long-expected attack on Mobile has at last begun, and that a large force is moving against Selma and Montgomery. One of the largest armies yet massed by the North is investing Richmond; Sherman and his vandals are in the very heart of the country, and a large army coming in by Wilmington—which is now in their hands; Charleston is closely besieged. Not one ray of light gleams from any quarter. It seems like hoping against hope; but my strong faith in the justice of our cause makes failure to me an impossibility.[14]

A few weeks later, after learning that Confederate president Jefferson Davis was captured, she wrote, "The patriot is now a prisoner."[15]

The war was over. Cumming returned to Mobile, where she was active in church, community activities, the United Daughters of the Confederacy, and the United Confederate Veterans. She never married. After her death on June 5, 1909, she was buried at Saint John's Episcopal Church in Mobile.

AFTER THE CIVIL WAR

9

After the war, many of the women who had volunteered as nurses returned to their families. A great number left the hospitals with little or no money, weakened health, and exhausted bodies. Unlike soldiers who had earned military pensions for their wartime service, these women were not legally entitled to benefits. Some wrote memoirs or lectured about their wartime experiences. Others worked to reestablish lives, fading into obscurity in the historical record of the war. However, the last of the soldiers were not

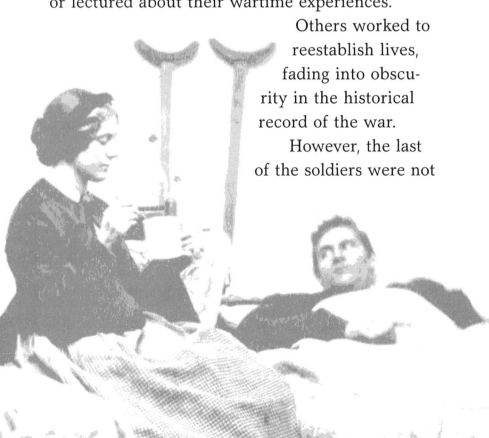

discharged until 1866, and some nurses stayed on at army hospitals until this time. In the South, nurses such as Phoebe Yates Pember provided valuable continuity in care as control of hospitals changed from Confederate to Federal authority.

Even after the close of army hospitals, some former nurses looked for new opportunities for helping soldiers. Some, like Sally L. Tompkins, nursed veterans in rehabilitation centers. Clara Barton searched for missing soldiers and sought to identify others who had died.

Other former nurses turned their efforts to the assistance of newly freed slaves, as teachers or as organizers of relief efforts. They organized schools or classes and gathered donations for the "freedmen," many of whom were now homeless. Deserted army camps became the first living quarters for many freed blacks. Former nurses collected supplies from charitable organizations in New England and distributed them to Southern blacks in need.

As the years passed, some nurses obtained government pensions in connection to their wartime service. In 1886, Mary Ann Bickerdyke was granted a monthly pension of $25. Dr. Mary Edwards Walker, whose eyesight was permanently damaged during her months in a

Confederate prison, had at first been granted a monthly disability pension of $8, which by 1899 was raised to $20. In 1892, a bill was passed granting a monthly pension of between $6 and $10 to nurses who could legally prove their wartime service. To the disappointment of many, their status as volunteers made it impossible to prove they had served.

In the years following the war, a few accounts were written about women's war efforts. One of these was by Mary Livermore, a nurse and executive in the U. S. Sanitary Commission. Livermore had regularly traveled from hospital to hospital during the war, recording observations about women's contributions to the war effort—both in and out of hospitals. In 1887,

Mary Ashton Livermore (1820–1905) is pictured in this undated portrait. Thanks to Livermore, women doctors and nurses of the Civil War will be remembered for their services to their country.

Two wounded soldiers receive care and medicine from Anne Bell, a Confederate Civil War nurse from Tennessee. This is an undated photograph taken sometime during the Civil War.

she published *My Story of the War: A Woman's Narrative of Four Years Personal Experience.* Published in 1867, one of the earliest accounts was written by Dr. L. P. Brocket and Mary C. Vaughan and titled *Women at War: A Record of Their Patriotic Contributions, Heroism, Toils and Sacrifice During the Civil War.* In a series of vignettes, the authors describe the notable work of nurses including Mary Ann Bickerdyke, Cornelia Hancock, and others. Hancock is introduced as being "among the most zealous and untiring of the women who ministered to the wounded men 'at the front,' in the long and terrible campaign of the Army of the Potomac in 1864-5."[1] Brocket and Vaughan's closing tribute to Hancock rings true for the entire body of women doctors and nurses: "This imperfect recognition is but a slight testimonial to the . . . untiring labors in behalf of sick and wounded soldiers."[2]

TIMELINE

1860 – Abraham Lincoln is elected president.

1860–1861 – Eleven Southern states secede from the Union, forming the Confederate States of America.

February 1861 – Jefferson Davis is inaugurated as president of the Confederacy.

April 12, 1861 – Confederate soldiers fire on Fort Sumter.

July 1861 – First Battle of Bull Run (Battle of Manassas).

August 1861 – Battle of Wilson's Creek.

March 1862 – Battle between the ships *Monitor* and *Merrimack* (Battle of the *Virginia*).

April 1862 – Battle of Shiloh.

June–July 1862 – Seven Days' Battle.

August 1862 – Second Battle of Bull Run (Second Battle of Manassas).

September 1862 – Battle of Antietam.

October 1862 – Battle of Perryville.

December 1862 – Battle of Fredericksburg.

January 1, 1863 – Emancipation Proclamation.

May 1863 – Battle of Chancellorsville.

May–July 1863 – Siege of Vicksburg, Mississippi.

June 1863 – Battle of Brandy Station.

July 1863 – Battle of Gettysburg.

November 1863 – Battle of Chattanooga.

August 1864 – Battle of Mobile Bay.

September 1864 – General Sherman captures Atlanta.

October 1864 – Battle of Cedar Creek.

November 1864	Lincoln is reelected president.
November–December 1864	General Sherman's 300-mile (483 km) "March to the Sea" from Atlanta to the Atlantic Ocean destroys anything useful to the Confederates.
April 2, 1865	Union forces capture Richmond, Virginia, the Confederacy's capital.
April 9, 1865	General Lee surrenders to General Grant at Appomattox Court House in Virginia.
April 14, 1865	President Lincoln is assassinated.
April–May 1865	Remaining Confederate forces surrender.
December 18, 1865	Thirteenth Amendment is ratified, abolishing slavery.

Glossary

abolition A movement to abolish, or end, slavery.

Civil War The conflict from 1861 to 1865 between the Northern states (the Union) and the Southern states (the Confederacy), which seceded from the Union.

Confederacy The eleven Southern states that seceded from the United States in 1860 and 1861; the South. Members of the Confederacy were called Confederates.

field hospital A temporary hospital set up near a field of battle.

matron A head nurse.

mobile hospital A hospital that moves to follow along with troops.

secede To withdraw from an organization; as a noun, *secession.*

Union Northern states loyal to the federal government headed by President Abraham Lincoln during the Civil War; the North. Members of the Union were called Federals.

United States Sanitary Commission The organization created by an order of President Abraham Lincoln to train nurses and improve sanitary conditions for the Union army.

veteran A former soldier.

98

For More Information

The Civil War Preservation Trust
1331 H Street NW, Suite 1001
Washington, DC 20005
(202) 367-1861
e-mail: info@civilwar.org
Web site: http://www.civilwar.org

The Museum of the Confederacy
1201 East Clay Street
Richmond, VA 23219
(804) 649-1861
e-mail: info@moc.org
Web site: http://www.moc.org

The National Civil War Museum
One Lincoln Circle at Reservoir Park
P.O. Box 1861
Harrisburg, PA 17105-1861
(717) 260-1861
Web site: http://nationalcivilwarmuseum.org

U.S. Army Women's Museum
2100 Adams Avenue
Building P-5219
Fort Lee, VA 23801-2100
(804) 734-4326
e-mail: AWMWeb@lee.army.mil
Web site: http://www.awm.lee.army.mil

Washington Civil War Association
P.O. Box 3043
Arlington, WA 98223
(800) 260-5997
e-mail: rebgunner@elvis.com
Web site: http://www.wcwa.net

WEB SITES
Due to the changing nature of Internet links, the Rosen Publishing Group, Inc., has developed an online list of Web sites related to the subject of this book. This site is updated regularly. Please use this link to access the list:

http://www.rosenlinks.com/aww/dncw

For Further Reading

De Angelis, Gina. *Female Firsts in Their Fields: Science and Medicine.* Philadelphia: Chelsea House, 1999.

Eggleston, Larry G. *Women in the Civil War: Extraordinary Stories of Soldiers, Spies, Nurses, Doctors, Crusaders, and Others.* Jefferson, NC: McFarland and Co., 2003.

Hillstrom, Kevin, and Laurie Collier Hillstrom. *American Civil War Biographies.* 2 volumes. Lawrence W. Baker, ed. Detroit: UXL Gale Group, 2000.

Levin, Beatrice. *Women and Medicine.* 3rd ed. Lanham, MD: Scarecrow Press, 2002.

Mikaelian, Allen. *Medal of Honor: Profiles of America's Military Heroes from the Civil War to the Present.* New York: Hyperion, 2002.

Savage, Douglas J. *Women in the Civil War.* Philadelphia: Chelsea House, 2000.

Wilbur, C. Keith. *Civil War Medicine 1861–1865.* Philadelphia: Chelsea House, 1995.

Bibliography

Alcott, Louisa May. *Hospital Sketches*. Cambridge, MA: Belknap Press, 1960.

Baker, Nina Brown. *Cyclone in Calico: The Story of Mary Ann Bickerdyke*. Boston: Little, Brown, 1952.

Beers, Fannie A. *Memories: A Record of Personal Experience and Adventure During Four Years of War*. Philadelphia: J. B. Lippincott, 1889.

Beller, Susan Provost. *Confederate Ladies of Richmond*. Brookfield, CT: Twenty-first Century Books, 1999.

Brocket, L. P., and Mary C. Vaughan. *Women at War: A Record of Their Patriotic Contributions, Heroism, Toils and Sacrifice During the Civil War*. Stamford, CT: Longmeadow, 1993.

Chang, Ina. *A Separate Battle: Women and the Civil War*. New York: Lodestar Books, 1991.

Cumming, Kate. *Kate: The Journal of a Confederate Nurse*. Richard Barksdale Harwell, ed. Baton Rouge, LA: Louisiana State University Press, 1959.

Dannett, Sylvia G., ed. *Noble Women of the North*. New York: Thomas Yoseloff, 1959.

Denney, Robert E. *Civil War Medicine: Care and Comfort of the Wounded*. New York: Sterling Publishing, 1994.

Doherty, Kieran. *Congressional Medal of Honor Recipients*. Springfield, NJ: Enslow Publishers, 1998.

Dubowski, Cathy East. *Clara Barton: Healing the Wounds*. Englewood Cliffs, NJ: Silver Burdett Press, 1991.

Hawks, Esther Hill. *A Woman Doctor's Civil War*. Gerald Schwartz, ed. Columbia, SC: University of South Carolina Press, 1984.

Hillstrom, Kevin, and Laurie Collier Hillstrom. *American Civil War Almanac*. Lawrence W. Baker, ed. Detroit: UXL Gale Group, 2000.

Hillstrom, Kevin, and Laurie Collier Hillstrom. *American Civil War Biographies*. 2 volumes. Lawrence W. Baker, ed. Detroit: UXL Gale Group, 2000.

Kent, Jacqueline C. *Women in Medicine*. Minneapolis: Oliver Press, 1998.

Levin, Beatrice. *Women and Medicine*. 3rd ed. Lanham, MD: Scarecrow Press, 2002.

Livermore, Mary A. *My Story of the War*. New York: Arno Press, 1972.

Maher, Mary Denis. *To Bind Up the Wounds: Catholic Sister Nurses in the U.S. Civil War*. Baton Rouge, LA: Louisiana State University Press, 1989.

Marshall, Helen E. *Dorothea Dix: Forgotten Samaritan*. New York: Russell and Russell, 1967.

Mikaelian, Allen. *Medal of Honor: Profiles of America's Military Heroes from the Civil War to the Present*. New York: Hyperion, 2002.

Oates, Stephen B. *A Woman of Valor: Clara Barton and the Civil War*. New York: Free Press, 1994.

Pember, Phoebe Yates. *A Southern Woman's Story: Life in Confederate Richmond*. Bell Irvin Wiley, ed. St. Simons Island, GA: Mockingbird Books, 1959.

Sanitary Commission of the United States Army: A Succinct Narrative of Its Works and Purposes. New York: Arno Press, 1972.

Schleichert, Elizabeth. *The Life of Dorothea Dix*. Frederick, MD: Twenty-first Century Books, 1992.

Sherrow, Victoria. *Women and the Military: An Encyclopedia*. Denver, CO: ABC-CLIO, 1996.

Wilbur, C. Keith. *Civil War Medicine 1861–1865*. Philadelphia: Chelsea House, 1995.

Source Notes

Introduction
1. Fannie A. Beers, *Memories: A Record of Personal Experience and Adventure During Four Years of War* (Philadelphia: J. B. Lippincott, 1889), p. 81.
2. Ibid., p. 80.

Chapter 1
1. Elizabeth Schleichert, *The Life of Dorothea Dix* (Frederick, MD: Twenty-first Century Books, 1992), p. 70.
2. Ibid., p. 13.
3. Ina Chang, *A Separate Battle: Women and the Civil War* (New York: Lodestar Books, 1991), p. 36.

Chapter 2
1. Phoebe Yates Pember, *A Southern Woman's Story: Life in Confederate Richmond*, Bell Irvin Wiley, editor (St. Simons Island, GA: Mockingbird Books, 1959), p. 2.
2. Ibid., p. 16.
3. Ibid.
4. Ibid., p. 15.
5. Ibid.
6. Ibid., p. 17.

7. Ibid., pp. 24–25.
8. Ibid., p. 25.
9. Louisa May Alcott, *Hospital Sketches* (1863), (Cambridge, MA: Belknap Press, 1960), p. 60.
10. Pember, p. 25.
11. Ibid., p. 19.
12. Ibid., p. 21.
13. Ibid., p. 6.
14. Ibid.
15. Ibid., p. 8.
16. Ibid., p. 62.

Chapter 3

1. Esther Hill Hawks, *A Woman Doctor's Civil War*, Gerald Schwartz, editor (Columbia, SC: University of South Carolina Press, 1984), p. 49.
2. Ibid.
3. Ibid., p. 7.
4. Ibid., p. 38.
5. Ibid., p. 49.
6. Ibid., p. 50.
7. Ibid., p. 51.
8. Ibid.
9. Ibid., p. 53.
10. Ibid., pp. 53–54.
11. Ibid., p. 71.
12. Ibid., p. 68.
13. Ibid., p. 129.

Chapter 4

1. Beatrice Levin, *Women and Medicine*, 3rd ed. (Lanham, MD: Scarecrow Press, 2002), p. 84.
2. Sylvia G. Dannett, editor, *Noble Women of the North* (New York: Thomas Yoseloff, 1959), p. 232.
3. L. P. Brocket and Mary C. Vaughan, *Women at War: A Record of Their Patriotic Contributions, Heroism, Toils and Sacrifice During the Civil War* (1867), reprinted (Stamford, CT: Longmeadow, 1993), pp. 172–173.
4. Ibid., p. 173.
5. Levin, p. 85.
6. Mary Elizabeth Massey, *Bonnet Brigades: American Women and the Civil War* (New York: Alfred A. Knopf, 1966), p. 49.
7. Brocket and Vaughan, p. 176.
8. Beatrice Levin, p. 85.

Chapter 5

1. Cathy East Dubowski, *Clara Barton: Healing the Wounds* (Englewood Cliffs, NJ: Silver Burdett Press, 1991), pp. 66, 68.
2. Ibid., p. 18.
3. Ibid., p. 17.
4. Stephen B. Oates, *A Woman of Valor: Clara Barton and the Civil War* (New York: Free Press, 1994), p. 5.
5. Dubowski, p. 47.
6. Ibid., p. 53.

Chapter 6

1. Allen Mikaelian, *Medal of Honor: Profiles of America's Military Heroes from the Civil War to the Present* (New York: Hyperion, 2002), p. 1.
2. Ibid., p. 6.
3. C. Keith Wilbur, *Civil War Medicine 1861–1865* (Philadelphia: Chelsea House, 1995), p. 45.
4. Mikaelian, p. 7.
5. Karen Zeinert, *Those Courageous Woman of the Civil War* (Brookfield, CT: Millbrook Press, 1998), p. 49.
6. Mikaelian, p. xviii.

Chapter 7

1. Susan Provost Beller, *Confederate Ladies of Richmond* (Brookfield, CT: Twenty-first Century Books, 1999), p. 46.
2. Jane Stuart Woolsey, *Hospital Days: Reminiscence of a Civil War Nurse* (Roseville, MN: Edinborough Press, 1996), p. 21.
3. Thomas Cooper DeLeon, *Belles, Beaux, and Brains of the 60's* (New York: G. W. Dillingham Company, 1907), p. 389.

Chapter 8

1. Kate Cumming, *Kate: The Journal of a Confederate Nurse*, Richard Barksdale Harwell, editor (Baton Rouge, LA: Louisiana State University Press, 1959), p. xii.
2. Ibid., p. 12.
3. Ibid., p. 13.

4. Ibid., p. 14.
5. Ibid.
6. Ibid.
7. Ibid., p. 15.
8. Ibid.
9. Ibid., p. 40.
10. Ibid., p. 49.
11. Ibid., p. 111.
12. Ibid., p. 178.
13. Ibid., p. 179.
14. Ibid., p. 266.
15. Ibid., p. 284.

Chapter 9
1. L. P. Brocket and Mary C. Vaughan, *Women at War: A Record of Their Patriotic Contributions, Heroism, Toils and Sacrifice During the Civil War* (1867), reprinted (Stamford, CT: Longmeadow, 1993), p. 284.
2. Ibid., p. 286.

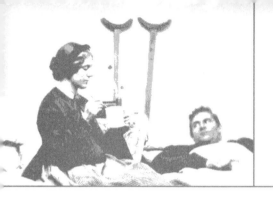

Index

110

About the Author

Lesli J. Favor enjoys writing about people and events that have shaped North America. Her books include *Francisco Vasquez de Coronado, The Iroquois Constitution,* and *Martin Van Buren.* Lesli earned her BA in English at the University of Texas at Arlington. She earned her MA and PhD from the University of North Texas and currently lives in Dallas.

Photo Credits

Front cover, pp. 7, 22–23, 29, 36, 47, 49, 54, 60, 61, 65, 70, 93 Library of Congress, Prints and Photographs Division; back cover, p. 56 National Museum of Health and Medicine, Washington, DC; pp. 10, 71, 76, 84, 94 © Corbis; p. 13 © Medford Historical Society Collection/Corbis; p. 15 University of Connecticut Libraries, Thomas J. Dodd Research Center, Josephine A. Dolan Collection; pp. 18, 45 Still Picture Branch, National Archives and Records Administration; p. 24 http://www.jewish-history.com; pp. 32, 85 General Research Division, New York Public Library, Astor, Lenox, and Tilden Foundations; p. 37 Library of Congress, Rare Book and Special Collections Division; p. 43 Reynolds Historical Library, the University of Alabama at Birmingham; p. 58 Culver Pictures; p. 69 Division of Social History, Political History, National Museum of American History, Smithsonian Institution, Behring Center, gift of Mrs. Jack Wilson; p. 74 © Museum of the City of New York/Corbis; pp. 77, 79 Museum of the Confederacy, Richmond, VA, photography by Katherine Wetzel; p. 88 Jean Rosales/KittyTours.

Designer: Evelyn Horovicz; **Editor:** Joann Jovinelly; **Photo Researcher:** Peter Tomlinson